From Heaven and Back Again

A collections of poems and musings on the Christian faith

Stewart French

authorHOUSE®

AuthorHouse™ UK Ltd.
500 Avebury Boulevard
Central Milton Keynes, MK9 2BE
www.authorhouse.co.uk
Phone: 08001974150

© 2011 Stewart French. All rights reserved.

No part of this book may be reproduced, stored in a retrieval system, or transmitted by any means without the written permission of the author.

First published by AuthorHouse 24/3/2011.

ISBN: 978-1-4567-7297-0 (sc)

Any people depicted in stock imagery provided by Thinkstock are models, and such images are being used for illustrative purposes only. Certain stock imagery © Thinkstock.

This book is printed on acid-free paper.

Because of the dynamic nature of the Internet, any Web addresses or links contained in this book may have changed since publication and may no longer be valid. The views expressed in this work are solely those of the author and do not necessarily reflect the views of the publisher, and the publisher hereby disclaims any responsibility for them.

This book contains some of the poems and articles written over a twenty year period, which reflect the way I felt about issues to do with the Christian faith, with my response to Jesus, or concerns that were dear to my heart when I put pen to paper.

My thanks for constant encouragement in writing - as in everything else - go, naturally enough, first to God and then to my wife Gwen, to my parents and to my children. Beyond that small circle, I would add the ministers who were primarily responsible for the combined United Reformed / Methodist church in Ashford in which we worshipped over the years when the majority of these were written (Richard Davis, Ted Bishop and Jeremy Dare), and also those who faithfully prepared the local Methodist Circuit Magazines in Chippenham and Ashford where these first saw the light of day

Finally, there are many others, too numerous to mention by name, who in many different ways have helped and encouraged me, and those who have sat with my wife and me as I have been through many 'dark nights of the soul', have faced fears and feelings from my past, and have come out the other side.

Stewart French

October 2010

SUBJECT INDEX

PART 1 CHRISTMAS p 1

The greatest story ever told starts in a simple manger - an age-old story, which loses nothing by repetition. We who are within the Church hear it so often that we can overlook the deeper meaning, whilst for many outside the Church family, it means nothing anyway except for the opportunity to 'splash out' and have a party.

If only I knew how to tell them...

PART 2 CALVARY AND EASTER p 12

This section deals with that which is absolutely central to our faith, the crucifixion of Jesus at the hands of men. It is pivotal to all that God planned, but so often I seem to 'take it for granted' and need to be reminded of the ugliness of the crucifixion, the utter squalor of the cross, and the pain it caused both the Father and the Son.

Fortunately for us, the Resurrection followed soon after...

PART 3 AFTER CALVARY p 25

The events at Calvary were not the end, more 'the end of the beginning'. They led to other aspects of Jesus' ministry, and to promises for us which are still being unfolded...

PART 4   PERSONAL POEMS   p 31

As I assume the majority of ministry springs as much from personal experiences as from revelation and teaching, much of what I write has its roots in experiences throughout my life. I was privileged to be born into a loving, caring, Christian family, but the world has not always been so kind...

PART 5   THE CHURCH'S MISSION   p 50

Jesus told us to go and make disciples of all men everywhere. How we do that will very much depend upon both our individual characters and experiences, and also the type of Church where God has put us...

PART 6   OTHER POEMS   p 76

The items included here do not fit into any particular bracket, but I include them anyway...

PART 7   ARTICLES AND APHORISMS   p 92

I have included a few articles and playlets written over the years. You may find them of help.

"HELLO MARY, THIS IS JOE"

Many of us know the story of the Annunciation, how Mary received the momentous news that would change the world. I have often wondered how she might break the news to Joseph in the 20th century, with mobile telephones and all the other items we take for granted........

In this sketch please feel free to add pauses (I originally wrote 'pregnant pauses') at appropriate times.

Joseph tries to ring Mary, but gets the 'Engaged' tone. He taps his foot in frustration.

"Typical woman, always on the phone."

Keeps trying until he gets through.

"Hey Mary, its me. Joe."

"What was that? "Joe who?" I'm your fiancé for Heaven's sake, the one you're going to marry next year. Anyway, you know that United versus Liverpool match at Old Trafford you wanted to go to in about six months? Good news, I've got the tickets!"

"What do you mean, you don't know if you'll be able to come? Be consistent Woman, you've been bending my ear to get the tickets for ages now. And it is six months away still"

"Pardon? - Did I hear you right? - Not in your condition?"
"You don't mean...? You do mean..., don't you?"

"Let me understand a bit... Do I know the father? ... What do you mean "Sort of?""

"Okay, then, lets have all the sordid details, bit by bit."

"I see...It was an angel!...Of course, Darling, I should have guessed."

"But he didn't touch you? Naturally!... That's how it always happens...in fairy stories anyway.. Darling."

"Do I believe you? Of course I do...NOT! If that's how you carry on behind my back, as far as I am concerned, the wedding's off. Goodbye!"

He slams down telephone in anger and hurt.

Of course, we know that that is not how it ended. I often think that one of the greatest miracles at Christmas was how God changed Joseph's heart and mind, and how Joseph became so 100% protective of Mary and his stepson.

*

AND SO THIS IS CHRISTMAS

I find the opening words of the record "Merry Xmas, War is Over" by the late John Lennon a real challenge. The concept of the meaning of Christmas expressed in his record may be poles apart from my understanding, but I thank God for the way that John Lennon was able put into words what so many people think:-

"And so this is Christmas, and what have we done?
Another year over, and a new one just begun."

These words seem to me to sum up the hopelessness of Christmas without Jesus at the centre, shaping and changing our lives. Whilst using his opening words for a title, I hope that my words, written in 1991, may sum up the meaning of Christmas in a very different way.

Is this what Christmas really means, the fighting in the queues[1]
To buy expensive presents, or to stock up well with booze?
Down to the finest detail, our Christmas must be planned,
Forgetting poor and lonely folk, living near at hand.

Presents must be posted off, the turkey bought and cooked.
We must be so organised with nothing overlooked.
All our thoughts and efforts are being geared towards 'that day'
Forgetting poor and hungry folk, half a world away.

Is Christmas really just about this mad, commercial whirl?
What happened to the innocence we knew as boy or girl?
It's a common fallacy that 'No money means no joy',
Forgetting Christmas started with a naked, baby boy.

Are we too late to recapture the innocence that's flown?
How can we ever know again the joy that we have known?
Let's gaze again at Bethlehem, on that scene forever new,
Remembering God's word to us, "Here is my gift, to you."

*

[1] NB: for our American friends, "queues" are what you refer to as "lines"

CHRISTMAS IS FAST APPROACHING

Commercialism rears its head in the build up to each Christmas, and the real meaning of the Nativity - that of God speaking to His world - seems to be lost.

Christmas is fast approaching and the lights are burning bright;
"Come and buy your presents here, morning, noon and night."
The Royal Mail is gearing up to cope with increased load,
And credit cards are God's good gift to cope with what is owed.
But amidst the noise and chaos, a gentle voice is heard:
"My child, remember me!"

The cards must all be written now, with annual letters sent.
The Christmas bonus from the firm will very soon be spent.
The long shut down at work arrives, the factory quietens down,
And all 'the lads' frequent the pubs in every part of town.
But amidst the noise and bustle, that gentle voice is heard:
"My child, remember me!"

Two thousand years have come and gone since Gabriel spoke her name:
"Mary! God's child will be your son; things will never be the same".
He came to lead a perfect life, but He died a sinner's death
And opened Heaven's door to us, with His triumphant dying breath.
His is the voice that whispers still, that is trying to be heard,
"Do you remember Me?"

*

A HYMN FOR CHRISTMAS

This was written in 1996. I had recently been reading the book of Isaiah, and I had been struck by what he prophesied about the coming Lord.

How could he have known?

(Sung to the tune of "Maccabaeus", commonly associated with "Thine Be The Glory")

----

1) Born to a Virgin, in a stable bare,
   Jesus, Son of Heaven, our life came to share.
   You who left the Heavens, for this world of hurt,
   Started life's existence amidst filth and dirt.

*Chorus: We come to worship, helpless baby boy,
    Lost in adoration, our hearts full of joy.*

2) Isaiah foretold, to a Virgin born
   Earth's creator helpless, that first Christmas morn.
   Kings came as did shepherds, to that manger stall
   We now come as they did - listening to your call.

*Chorus: We come to worship, helpless baby boy,
    Lost in adoration, our hearts full of joy.*

3) Your life was offered, on that awful hill:
   Dying, as in living, following God's will.
   Through your resurrection death has lost its sting -
   Proving Baby Jesus to be Christ the King,

*Chorus: We come to worship, helpless baby boy,
   Lost in adoration, our hearts full of joy.*

4) Lord, we would offer all we have to you.
   With our lives Lord Jesus, do what you would do,
   Put us where you want us, help us Lord to care,
   Strengthened by your Spirit, your love we would share.

*Chorus: We come to worship, helpless baby boy,
   Lost in adoration, our hearts full of joy.*

*

THE ADVERT AND THE TELEVIEWER

Sometimes commercialism in its many guises makes me angry. This poem, which seems to fit into this section for its comments on our materialistic society, was written for the Methodist Circuit Arts Festival shortly after we moved to Ashford. Writing it gave me a chance to let off steam...

The time has come, the adverts try
To sell you many things.
Cigars, and booze (with V.A.T.)
And necklaces, and rings.
You do not need to pay with cash
Use credit card, no strings.

It's all to do with what you want
And not with what you need.
We want to make you envious
To fill your mind with greed;
We aim to make you spend your cash,
And know we will succeed.

"When will you take your summer break?
And where will you go to?
You surely won't be staying here?
That's not the thing to do.
So come to us, we'll help you choose
Let us sell one to you."

"Your record player's getting old
You need a new T.V.
You ought to buy a video
And why not a CD?
Buy it quick whilst offers last
And get it INTEREST-FREE."

"Your money isn't doing much
Left in the bank you know.
Invest with us, we'll earn you more
So you can watch it grow.
Our rates are best, above the rest
As our statistics show."

The adverts pay for programmes, though
Like 'Brookside' and the news.
So is it really worth the breaks
For toys, cigars and booze?
I cannot speak for you and so
I must leave you to choose.

The programme's over, now the ads
Are on the screen you see.
You have the choice of what to do -
So what is it to be?
To turn it off and have a chat?
Or switch to BBC?

With apologies to Lewis Carrol (The Walrus and the Carpenter)
*

AFTER THE BIG DAY

The Magi have gone from the stable,
The shepherds returned to the hill.
The angels have ceased their chorus of praise,
The infant is silent, and still.
And Mary, and Joseph, look down on God's Son:
Their Saviour, Redeemer, whose life has begun.

They cannot imagine the future,
The years spent in Egypt, exiled.
For all that they know is a feeling of joy
When they look at their still, silent, child.
And Mary, and Joseph, look down on God's Son:
The infant whose journey through life has begun.

This Jesus whom God had created
Whom Mary had felt in her womb.
How could they imagine, how could they conceive
Would one day arise from the tomb?
And Mary, and Joseph, look down on God's Son:
Whose Calvary journey had now just begun.

*

UPON THE CROSS

When writing this in 1993 I had originally intended to include a second verse, outlining my thoughts concerning the answer to the question posed. No matter how hard I tried, the words would not come. I was reminded of a couple of lines in a song by Bob Dylan:

> "Now I can't think for you, you'll have to decide
> Whether Judas Iscariot had God on his side".

I leave it to you to to make up your own minds, and ponder the question for yourselves.

Upon the cross with arms outstretched, His body wracked with pain,
The Son of God was crucified, the Son of God was slain.
The perfect, sinless, Saviour at whose word the storm was stilled
Who would not hurt a damaged reed[1], but who let Himself be killed.
He chose to make this sacrifice, He chose to come and die:
Have you ever looked into His face, and asked the question, "Why?"
Why did the God who made this earth, who holds heavens in His palms,
Choose to die at Calvary, on a cross with outstretched arms?

*

[1] This is a reference to Isaiah 42 v3

PALM SUNDAY- AND BEYOND

To a Jerusalem that's waiting, is where, not hesitating,
Rides Jesus Christ, seated on an ass.
The crowd seethes with expectation, there are cries of adoration
For Jesus Christ, riding on an ass.

The procession's now advancing, and the people - joyful - dancing
Before Jesus Christ, seated on an ass.
The cry "Hosanna"'s ringing, and the crowd - excited - singing
"Make way for Jesus, riding on an ass."

With the city gates in sight, His eyes - with tears - are bright,
The Lord Jesus Christ, seated on an ass.
He hangs His head, heartbroken, as anguished prayers are spoken
By Jesus Christ, crying on an ass.

At the outskirts of the city, with His heart so full of pity
The Lord Jesus Christ climbs down from that ass.
His objective is selected. Towards where God has been neglected
Strides Jesus Christ, descended from that ass.

Oblivious to the dangers Jesus throws out the money-changers
From the Temple "which shall be a House of Prayer"
In righteous anger Jesus seethes, "This is now a place of thieves -
This Temple which should be a house of prayer."

It was only five days after, when anger replaced laughter
That Jesus Christ was hung upon a cross.
As our Saviour met his fate, that same crowd looked on with hate
At Jesus Christ, hung upon a cross.

What caused the alteration, to hate from adoration
For Jesus Christ now hung upon a cross?
What was it in his actions that upset so many factions
And left Him there, naked on that cross?

As they'd looked into His eyes they could see no compromise
In Jesus Christ, the Father's only Son.
And things are still the same today, Jesus is the only way
We can only reach the Father through His Son

*

March 1998

GOOD FRIDAY- FROM MARY'S VIEWPOINT

If Good Friday is painful for us and was agony for Jesus, can you imagine how His mother must have felt? Whilst the Angel had warned her about how Jesus' life would develop, nothing anyone could have said could prepare any mother for what she saw that day.

"My God!" He cried as He hung there, His body lacerated.
"My God!"- again - Christ crucified by those He had created.
"Why have you forsaken me?" The scream reached to the skies
As He saw Heaven close its gates, through pain-occluded eyes.

His naked, beaten, body hung, with nails through hand and feet;
With crown of thorns upon His head, humiliation was complete.
His blood congealed in every wound, from whip, and nail, and thorn,
The Son of God, left hanging there, the object of men's scorn.

Now try and stand with Mary there. Look at Him on that cross.
Imagine feeling Mary's pain, or feel her sense of loss.
Her first-born son spread-eagled there, a thief on either side,
No wonder Mary's world collapsed, the day that Jesus died.

But Jesus knew that on the cross His victory would be won;
And with His dying breath He said "Woman, behold your son!"
When Mary looked into His eyes, she saw love there, undiminished
And heard His shout triumphant ring - "**TETALESTI!**"
[1] "**IT IS FINISHED!**"

*

[1] *"Tetalesti" is Aramaic for "It is finished".*

"THEY DIDN'T HALF HURT JESUS"

This was written in 1990 in response to an article by Adrian Plass in 'Family' Magazine from that year, where he described taking his son to see a 'real' picture of the Crucifixion, not one of the romanticised ones so often seen. His son's immediate reaction was

"They didn't half hurt Jesus, Dad"

which really spoke to me.

"They didn't half hurt Jesus, Dad,
See those thorns upon His head.
They must have been real sharp, Dad,
Can you see where Jesus bled?
Why did they do it, Dad?

They didn't half hurt Jesus, Dad,
Can you see His back's all scarred?
If they only used a whip, Dad,
They must have hit Him hard.
Why did they do it, Dad?

They didn't half hurt Jesus, Dad,
See Him stretched out in the sun.
Did they enjoy their 'sport' Dad?
And did they find it fun?
Why did they do it, Dad?

They didn't half hurt Jesus, Dad,
There's a spear hole in His side.
With all those things they did, Dad,
No wonder Jesus died.
Why did they do it, Dad?

They didn't half hurt Jesus, Dad,
Aren't they nails that I can see?
What are you trying to say, Dad?
He went through that for me?
Why are you crying, Dad?"

*

CRUCIFIED - FOR ME

Calvary was extremely painful, both for Jesus and for the Father.
To the Romans it was a routine.
To us it can mean eternity with God.

As Jesus died - with arms outstretched - His blood was running free;
That blood He chose to spill that day was shed for you and me.
They'd crowned Him with a wreath of thorns, they'd put nails through hands and feet
And hung him, naked, in the sun - Romans were not discrete.
A lingering death was what they sought, an example their objective,
And Jesus stayed there on that cross, subject to men's invective.

Twelve thousand angels stood aghast, they could not take it in:
Their Jesus, going to that cross, a man devoid of sin.
He trod the path that others feared; that agonising death;
They'd seen Him being whipped and scarred, they'd heard Him gasp for breath.
They saw the guards bang in those nails, they heard the soldiers cry
"He called Himself the Son of God. Let's watch Him slowly die."

"Forgive them, Father," Jesus called, as the soldiers did their worst

But one, at least, brought water when his Saviour cried "I thirst."

Could that soldier see forgiveness in that beaten, bloodied face?

Did he see his Saviour, Jesus Christ, was dying in his place?

What made that soldier different? Was that man the first to see

That Jesus' death was pre-ordained? That Jesus died for me?

*

EASTER - FROM MARY MAGDALENE'S VIEWPOINT

As she sat beside the open grave, poor Mary simply wept;
She didn't know who'd moved the stone, whilst Roman soldiers slept.
She couldn't know who'd moved the corpse, "It's gone" was all she knew
And head in hands she sat and wept, as you or I might do.

She had known His true forgiveness, she had heard Him speak her name.
Then seen Him on that awful cross, hung up to die in shame.
She had heard Him cry "Forsaken" as His Father turned His head:
What point was there in living now, when Jesus Christ was dead?

She then sensed a man beside her, despite her pain and grief.
The words of Christ "I will return" now seemed beyond belief.
She asked where they had laid Him, so that she could truly mourn,
How could she know what joy would flow from that first Easter dawn?

His voice cut through her sorrow: His words cut through her tears.
The voice she heard is speaking still - across two thousand years.
Throughout those years He's spoken, calling people back to God,
To walk the path that Mary walked, and to tread where Mary trod.

That each one should hear from Jesus, from our Lord once crucified,
From the Christ who is now risen and is at His Father's side;
Whose hands still bear the nail prints, and whose head the crown of thorn,
Who is speaking words of comfort still, as on that Easter dawn.

*

RESURRECTION JOY

In this attempt at hymn writing I tried to convey the events at the Tomb on that first Easter morning, and what they mean to us today.

*To the tune "St. Lawrence" (Hymns & Psalms 820)
or "Nativity" (Hymns & Psalms 821)*

Jesus is Lord, the devil's lost;
Beaten at Calvary.
Though Satan fights, Jesus has won;
He has the victory.

Jesus the Lord, to Mary came,
As she wept bitter tears.
Gently He spoke, He called her name,
And banished all her fears.

Jesus - her Lord - said "Tell my friends,
So they no longer grieve."
She went with joy, to give this news
But they would not believe.

Jesus - their Lord - appeared to them
Within the upper room.
Their hearts all rose, they realised
He had risen from the tomb.

Jesus our Lord, we know you are
Here and enthroned above.
Help us to share what we all know
Your care, our peace, your love.

Jesus my Lord I offer you
My life, my everything.
Please take it all Dear Risen One
My Lord. My God. My King.

Jesus - you're Lord: the devil's lost;
Beaten at Calvary.
Though he may fight, he cannot win;
You have the victory.

*

A PENTECOST EXPERIENCE

Different strands of Christian tradition seem to view the coming of the Holy Spirit in different ways - maybe that is not a bad thing as God has made us all different. No matter how you view Him, however, the Holy Spirit has a purpose.

Will you feel the Spirit coming as you wait in expectation?
Will you feel God's power coursing through your veins?
Or will the Spirit touch you in the areas where you're hurting?
Will you let Him loose those heavy, binding, chains?

The coming of God's Spirit can be like a bolt of lightning,
Or He can come to you as gentle as a dove.
But however you encounter Him, He comes with one intention,
So you can show the truth of Jesu's love.

The working of God's miracles, His deliverances and healings
Are to show the world the power of God today.
But God's not a magician scaring people to repentance,
To win them with His love's God's chosen way.

And the gifts the Spirit gives us are both manifold and varied
So we can serve God in this world of need.
And the fruit that grows within us will enable God to change us
So Christ is seen within the lives we lead.

The offer of God's Spirit has been made to all His people
Approach with faith and you will find it's true.
When you've received that touch from God, you'll find strength to accomplish
Whatever God's prepared for you to do.

So...

Did you feel the Spirit coming as you prayed in expectation?
Did you feel God's power coursing through your veins?
Or did the Spirit touch you in the areas where you're hurting?
Did you feel Him loose those heavy, binding, chains?

*

IF YOU HAVE TEARS

Many of us can remember learning Shakespeare at school. For 'O' level I studied "Julius Caesar", and I can still recall much of that wonderful series of speeches by Mark Anthony to the general population, one part of which begins with the words: "If you have tears.."

If you have tears prepare to shed them now – as you gaze on that scene in Eden;
Where Adam and Eve fail Satan's test;
Where Adam eats, at Eve's request:
"When we try this fruit we'll know what's best".
Prepare to shed them now.

If you have tears prepare to shed them now – as you look on that garden scene.
The Son of God, crying, weeping;
His chosen disciples, dozing, sleeping;
And Judas, his evil appointment keeping.
Prepare to shed them now.

If you have tears prepare to shed them now – as you view that courtyard scene;
The Son of Man, beaten, battered;
His frightened disciples, fleeing, scattered;
All their hopes and dreams lie shattered.
Prepare to shed them now.

If you have tears prepare to shed them now – as you look on Calvary's hill.
With His arms outstretched, fingers pointed;
God's only Son, His annointed;
Meeting His death, long appointed.
Prepare to shed them now.

If you have tears prepare to shed them now – as you see the empty tomb.
He is risen, death defeated;
Satan's forces have retreated;
See Christ in glory, where He's seated.
Now shed those tears of joy.

*

THE SECOND COMING

This particular poem was inspired by some teaching on the Book Of Revelation from David Pawson at the Full Gospel Business Men's Fellowship International weekend at Loughborough in 1997.

When the clouds will split asunder and the Son of God descend
Men will stand in awe and wonder as this age comes to its end:
Then He will judge all nations fairly - whether foe or whether friend -
When Jesus Christ returns to claim the earth.

Is your destiny with Jesus, has your salvation been assured?
Will you know His life eternal, there forever with the Lord?
Have you the full, complete forgiveness, which at Calvary was secured?
When Jesus died for all upon His earth.

Will you see your friends in Heaven, or will you be forever lost?
Do you know the peace that Jesus bought, at such tremendous cost?
Or are you just unstable, are you forever being tossed
By Satan's hosts assembled here on earth?

For the devil is an expert in both lying and deceit,
Who will take our pride as Christians and will turn it to conceit.
The ambitions that the devil has will never be complete
Until he's crowned as king of all the earth.

But Jesus did not die for that, to let the devil win;
Instead He died to set us free, to cancel all our sin.
And we can be strengthened daily by the Holy Ghost within
So we can show His power here on earth.

Are you living in that power, or does the devil have his way?
Does Jesus guide your every thought, or do Satan's hosts hold sway?
Do you trust in God to plan your life - does He have the final say
In all you do for Him upon His earth?

Does your life show your commitment to God's perfect, sinless Son?
Are you introducing people to the risen, living One?
Will you be prepared and ready when the final battle's won
And we - and He - return to rule God's earth?

*

WHY DOES GOD BOTHER WITH PEOPLE LIKE ME?

I was standing on the top of a local sand quarry, looking down at the rabbits below, and all I wanted to do was to jump and try to end it all. What stopped me was not the thoughts of my family, but simply the thought that I may only injure myself, and end up paralysed or crippled.
I wondered then, as I have often wondered since:

Why does God bother with people like me
Who can't take the world in our stride?
He wants us to know that He thinks we're O.K.
So why do we just run and hide?
Why does God bother with me?

Why does God bother with people like me
Who keep all the pain deep inside?
He wants us to tell Him the hurts in our lives
So why do we just run and hide?
Why does God bother with me?

Why does God bother with people like me
Whose lives are blighted with pride?
He wants us to lower the barriers down
So why do we just run and hide?
Why does God bother with me?

*

DOUBTS AND CERTAINTIES

This was written very soon after the previous poem, and reflects very much the way I was feeling – I had not trusted God, and so my doubts multiplied. Once I shared my doubts and frustrations with God things became clearer: it is amazing how much we can learn from the Psalms!

I wandered lonely with my doubts
Within a world God claimed as His.
And in my mind I saw my life -
Full of God's broken promises.
When others said He'd set them free
Why had my God deserted me?

But this was Satan's ploy for me
Not shake my faith, nor doubt the cross
But look within and get depressed
To see myself, my life, as dross.
To tell myself with certainty
"It isn't true that God loves me!"

I screamed at God and asked Him then -
If His free love was really true
Why was He hiding it from me?
He said "It isn't me, it`s you!
Your heart is cold, you just can't see!"
He asked me then, "Do you love me?"

I wandered renewed in my faith
And saw a world I knew was His
And deep within I knew my God
Would keep His glorious promises.
And in my heart, which now was free
I really knew that God loved me.

*

Aug 1990, with apologies to W. Wordsworth (Daffodils)

TO HELL AND BACK

I've been to Hell and back, my friend
To Hell and back I've been.
I've seen the devil and felt despair
Beneath that baleful, hateful glare
I felt as though God didn't care.
To Hell and back I've been.

My insides churned with fear and dread:
Withdrawn within my shell
I couldn't see where to begin,
For nobody could clear my sin
All Satan's army crowded in
When I was in my Hell.

But in my darkest hour, my friend
When things were really black,
Friends came to talk, and those friends stayed,
And those friends laughed, and those friends prayed;
And slowly I felt less afraid
For I was coming back.

I've been to Hell and back, my friend,
For I'm the devil's loss.
I've walked away from Satan's claws
Turned from Hell's wide open doors,
I'm safe with God while life endures
Thanks to an empty cross.

*

FATHER YOU LOVE ME

This was written sometime around 1985. I wrote the first verse and Gwen, together with Anne Anderson, encouraged me to write a bit more. Originally it was meant to be sung to the tune: "Father we love you"

Father you love me,
I know now that you love me.
I know it for you have shown me how.
Though I've felt alone
I've not been on my own
And Father God I really know that now.

Jesus I'm pure now,
My sins they are no more now
From sin and from guilt you've set me free.
Taking all my pain,
All my hurt and shame,
You bled and you died for only me.

Spirit I'm free now
To be what I should be now.
I'm free from the past and all my fears.
My life's begun anew,
I'm walking close with you,
I know you will restore those blighted years.

*

REJECTION

This was written in 1991, and I believe it speaks for itself.
Maybe someone reading this can relate to it.

Why do we feel like giving up on work for which we're called?
Why do we feel we're all alone, just us against the world?
Could it be, when things get tough, that we lose God's protection?
Or, maybe, others keep away, and so we feel rejection.

Folk never just 'drop by' or ring, to let us know they care;
To let us open up, or laugh, or spend a time in prayer.
We all have need of company, of spending time with others
For that's God's purpose for His church, to care for all our brothers.

It seems to take a crisis time for us to let tears flow.
It`s then that others realise our 'mask' is just for show.
Behind those composed, steady, lips, words desperate to be spoken,
Our eyes are wet, our courage gone, our spirit nearly broken.

That's why we feel like giving up, because we live a lie,
That says that "We must carry on, for Christians never cry."
And in our lives, with all our hurts, emotion's never shown.
For we've been schooled for many years to do it on our own.

Why should I let my barriers down and show you what's inside?
I must maintain appearances, because I have my pride.
It is hard for me to let you know what's eating at my heart,
But whilst I don't Rejection will keep tearing me apart.

*

A FRIEND

This was written in December 1996, shortly after my father died. One day my mother expressed the sentiment "She's a real friend" about another lady who had been a dog-walker, a listener and a willing volunteer for everything that was needed. All her life my mother (like her mother before her) has been just such a person to others, and it has been wonderful to see her rewarded in her time of need.

When life is not worth living and when your hopes have all but died;
When tomorrow is a burden, and when all today you've cried;
When the future seems so empty that you want to run and hide:-
That's when you need a friend.

When your plans are all collapsing and you don't know what to do;
When you feel the pressure crowding in and life's abandoned you;
When there's no-one there to share the load or tell you what to do:-
That's when you need a friend.

When your home is far from happy and your family life's a strain:-
When your marriage was a failure and you're left with guilt and pain:-
When you see your children's faces but you just cannot explain:-
That's when you need a friend.

When you've just been made redundant and the money's all but gone:-
When life itself seems hopeless, and there's no point in going on:-
When there's nothing left in all the world to build your hopes upon:-
That's when you need a friend.

A friend will not reject you, though there are things he can't condone:-
A friend will always be there, so you will not be left alone:-
For it's in the hard times - not the good - that friendship's really shown!
Could you be someone's friend?

*

IGNORED BY GOD?

My wife and I know that God heals; we have seen Him heal others, sometimes miraculously. We also know that deliverance is real, as we have both experienced it for ourselves. What I found very hard to bear at the end of 1997 was that for two years we had prayed - along with many others - for our daughter, Hazel, that her wrist would be healed, but without success. On the day she was due for her operation, after two long years of almost constant pain, she had a temperature of 103°F, and the operation had to be postponed. I felt that we were outside God's 'area of concern', and my faith was severely tested. Although many stood by us, I was struggling. As so often happens, it was when I put my thoughts into verse that I seemed to receive an answer from God.

Specific prayers not answered, and the disappointment's real.
I wonder "Can the Father really know the way I feel?
How can He sit in heaven, and pretend He cares for all
When He doesn't seem to listen to His children when they call?"

When I look within the Scriptures I read God's word is true.
What God has promised faithfully, I read that He will do.
He promises to answer all His children when they pray,
So where is God when nothing's done? Perhaps He's looked away.

Perhaps His mind is occupied, perhaps He hasn't time.
Maybe He's busy somewhere else - an irony sublime.
It may just be that I don't count, that I'm not a special case,
Or maybe I was simply in the wrong time and wrong place.

Unimportant little me, I start to feel rejected
All alone, forgotten soul, forgotten and neglected.
The devil's having lots of fun and I have let him in,
For when I took my eyes off God, I let the devil win.

But God has His own timing, and we can't always see
The way that He has planned things out, the way they're meant to be.
I should embrace God's purpose, which includes a plan for all
And should know that He is listening to His children when we call.

*

DESPAIR

This poem written in January 1999 helped me through a personal, emotional crisis, the details of which are not relevant in this book. Suffice it to say that the title speaks for itself.

When you are in the depths of depression, and you can't lift your eyes from the floor,
When you've taken each blow that Satan can throw, and you feel you can't take any more,
When you're feeling the work that the Father has given has come to an unfinished end
You'll find Christ is at hand, and that He'll understand, and that with Him you needn't pretend.
When all that you strive for has crumbled away, and you feel that nothing remains,
When the people you trust have gone back on their word, and that just adds to your pains,
When all of your hope lies crushed at your feet, and the world seems hopeless and bleak
You'll find Jesus is near, He is ready to hear. He is also ready to speak.

He has heard it before, and will hear it again, how you feel you have failed in your task.
He has heard it before, so kneel down on the floor, Jesus suffered so you could ask
"Please will you strengthen me, please will You help. I have fallen short of Your plan.
You know the frustrations, You know how it hurts, for Jesus You once were a man.
You know what it's like when Your plans turn to dust, and 'aspiration's a thing You have known'
When hope disappears; when the mind fills with fears; when You feel completely alone.
Lord You knew it yourself, as You knelt on that night, and Your chosen ones all fell asleep -
Lord I feel like that too, Christ I cannot go on. I just want to lie down and weep."

When you've vented your feelings at Jesus like that, and exhausted all of your pain,
Listen to Him as He speaks to your needs. He will be real, and loving again.
He can take all your problems and deal with each one, but it is up to you to let go:
If you hold on too tight, He will not try to fight, but His peace is unable to flow.
It is only the issues you surrender to Him that He deals with and gives you relief,
That He takes and resolves, so the problems are His, releasing your burden of grief.
For that is the reason that God 'put on skin', to share our frustrations and pain,
So we can express all our hurts to our Lord, and let Him refresh us again

*

DRIFTING

I recall the first Praise Service I attended after I had moved to Ashford. I had been out of work for a year, and just left my family 100 miles away. The Minister's opening words were "I pray God will lead some of you into wilderness experiences."

Over the years since then I have had times of doubt, times of feeling distant from God; maybe that is why I enjoy the writings of Adrian Plass so much, as he faces up to those periods of 'dryness' and doubt which so many other writers seem to either ignore or to not experience.

Maybe the following may help someone going through such an experience.

Is God a distant memory, does His love seem so remote?
Do you struggle with the Bible, with the letter that He wrote?
Do you feel that you have drifted, that you can't get through in prayer?
"Relax, my child, remember that your Father's always there."

Are you questioning the issues that you once believed as fact?
If you ask Him for an answer, does God seem so slow to act?
Do you wonder if your being here is thanks to God at all?
"Relax, my child, remember, I will answer when you call".

Do the sermons on a Sunday now all seem so dull and dry?
And the speakers can't get through to you, no matter how they try?
And no matter what you try to sing, the excitement isn't there?
"Relax, my child, remember, you are always in My care."

Can you recollect old feelings, "I am His and He is mine"?
Maybe around the table, as you shared the bread and wine.
Then open up your Bible and hear God's implicit vow
"Thus far have I led you, I will not forsake you now!"

*

THE HELPING HAND

This was written with Phil Osborne, then a Prison Officer and fellow member of the Ashford Chapter of the Full Gospel Business Men's Fellowship International.

"I despise myself, there's nothing here that anyone could love.
I'm just a total, useless waste of time.
And you - out there - can't understand what's going on inside,
As even I don't know what's in my mind.

I just can't take these pressures that are building up inside,
I'm ready to lash out, or shout, or scream.
I just don't know what's going on, I'm feeling so alone
God! Let it all be just an awful dream."

*"True inner peace will not be found in cigarettes or drugs
It can't be found in anything you take.
It only comes from knowing that you're valued for yourself,
That someone wants you just for your own sake.*

*You may succeed in 'blotting out' the world by getting drunk,
Or 'High' or in perhaps some other way.
But when you 'come to' from 'tripping out' your problems are still there,
The issues will not simply go away."*

"How can I find this 'inner peace' to calm my raging mind?
Where can I turn and not be pushed aside?
I've tried it all, and nothing works, I'm still all screwed up within,
There's no escape route left I haven't tried."

*"True 'inner peace', perfect peace, which can only come from Me
Can calm your heart and let your mind be still.
To receive it is not easy, though, you must lay aside your pride,
And walk up to that cross upon a hill.*

*At my cross, my friend, is your only chance to shed your heavy load:
The hurts, the pains, what's 'eating you' inside.
Then walk away with the past forgiven, and life begun afresh -
For that's the reason that I lived and died."*

*

REACH OUT

Reach out your hand to Jesus, He will never let you down,
He'll give you all the love your heart could crave.
He's standing right beside you, He's alive for evermore,
Not rotting in some Middle Eastern grave.

Whenever you are lonely, whenever tears may come,
Whatever needs you have, He's always there.
He is love incarnate, Jesus always understands
When no-one else around you seems to care.

His heart is overflowing with compassion for the weak,
The lonely, the neglected, those in pain.
He is forever interceding with the Father for your soul,
Whilst Satan tries to drag you down again.

So keep your eyes on Jesus, and focus on His love,
The love He gives, He gives for all to share.
Don't keep it all for your own needs, just take what you require
And use the rest to show how much you care.

This compassion for our brothers is what the Father gives
When we come to Him on humble, bended knee
And say "Father I'm a sinner; through the blood of Jesus Christ
Forgive, accept and then please set me free."

*"You are now free to love your neighbour in the love that Jesus gives,
Free to forgive the wrongs they've done to you.
Because, as my disciple, those things now lie in the past -
In your former life, for you've been born anew.*

*So celebrate your freedom by reaching out to Christ,
And take His hand and feel His love flow in.
Let Him take on all your sadness, let Him take on all your pain
Just as, at Calvary, He took all your sin."*

*

STANDING - ON HIS PROMISES?

I wrote this in one evening, after meditating on the opening line for many weeks. It struck me that we in the Church are very good at standing firm on the things that are precious to us, whilst maybe they are not always the things that are most precious to God.

Maybe, just maybe, however, I wrote this about me and my own apathy...

There's a world out there that is going to Hell, and the devil is rubbing his hands,
Whilst the Church, which is meant to bring sinners to Christ, instead of advancing, just stands.
"We'll stand for tradition, where nothing can change, we'll preserve an unchanging scene.
No new innovations, no modernist things, we shall be as we always have been.
Fresh people who enter our church must conform, for we're unable to alter our views:
So any new members must just settle down, and take their place in the pews.
We know what must happen on each Sunday here, we cannot accept what is new;
And there's no reason to think that God will show up, or will do what God used to do."

"Please, please, my dear children, let Me come in and stand alongside you all,
To strengthen your faith, to carry your load, and to lift you whenever you fall.
I know your intentions are all to the good, preserving a faith which is pure -
To pass on to others the truths which you know, in a way that makes you secure.
But standing like statues is not my intent, my church should move in my plan.
Look outward - not inward - and see the world's hurt, then act whenever you can.
You are my chosen to put things to right, my chosen to speak in my name.
I offer you power to go in my cause, it's there if only you'd claim.

But you're bound up with rituals, you're bound up with fear, those chains are keeping me out;
So how can I enter? How can I come in? How can I remove all your doubt?
How can I convince you I still move today, I've not sat back and watched from afar,
*And get you involved in **my** world today, if you're determined to stay as you are?*
I want you to listen, I want you to act, to have vision outside these four walls -
So pay heed to my Spirit, respond to His voice, obedient whenever He calls.
Remember the world that is going to Hell, for the devil is taking his chance.
Now! Will you stay standing where you always have been? Or can we - together - advance?"

*

WITHOUT A VISION....

*In April 1999 I was listening to an old tape from Spring Harvest, entitled "**Puppets**", and it made me very angry: angry at myself for my apathy, angry for the way I compromise, and angry for the way in which I do that which I <u>think</u> God wants, often without asking Him first.*

If this, the longest poem I have written to date, speaks to you, then I am pleased. Mainly it spoke to me and allowed me to get things off my chest.

"We need a vision, Father, on which we can focus as we pray
To give us our direction, so we don't drift from day to day.
We so soon become complacent and we forget the world outside
Where hate and fear are commonplace, and where love has been denied;
Where children are neglected and where old folk are forsaken -
And marriage vows are seldom kept - that's if they have been taken.
As Jesus cried "Forgive them for they know not what they do"
So we ask for mercy, that we have not heard from you."

We have not heard from Father because we have not thought to ask
"What purpose has God planned for us, what's our specific task?"
The Father's plan is not that we should simply drift along
But with our spirits blazing we should challenge what is wrong.
Christ did not die to make us "nice" but to start a revolution
Where we would fight for what is right, and offer His solutions.
But are we prepared to pay the price, and face the opposition
When we proclaim, without reserve, that "<u>This</u> is God's position!"

The world outside will tolerate a Church that meets each week
As long as we will compromise, and are afraid to speak,
Or act against injustice, or to say the world is wrong -
And watch them on their way to Hell, that vast ungospelled throng.
But does it really matter what the world thinks after all?
Is our 'hearing' now so muffled we can't hear the Spirit's call?
The Saviour is still praying that His church won't compromise
But will see the world, both good and bad, through the Creator's eyes.

Can we imagine how the Father feels as we gather "in His name"
Bent on maintaining silence so the world will stay the same.
Injustice won't be challenged, and children still will be abused
The homeless sleeping in the streets, but we won't be accused
Of speaking out against such things: of that there is no fear
"Leave us alone to meet each week, we're comfortable in here:
We've no desire to get involved, we have chosen not to know.
We'll keep the peace, not rock the boat. We'll maintain the status quo."

But that's not God's intention, that's not why the Saviour came.
He's calling us to action, to speak out in Jesus' name.
Where compromise is cowardice, as a Church are we prepared
To speak up for the victim, for the lonely and the scared?
To speak up for the unborn child, to say "Life is never cheap"
To tell the racist culture that "Skin colour's just skin deep"?
Are we willing to proclaim the truths enshrined within God's laws:
Go beyond just treating symptoms? All out attack upon the cause?

Maybe the purpose for this Church is not along these lines
But if each of us is half asleep we will never see the signs.
He calls us to be watchmen, to stand guard upon the walls,
To look with eyes wide open, and to hear Him when He calls.
Each fellowship is different, and each unique in many ways.
A multi faceted diamond, reflecting Heavenly rays -
God's church on earth is varied: what God wants is we conform
To His commands, to His design - United, not Uniform.

"We need this vision Father, so that we can see your plan
But help us sort out what's from you, rejecting what's from man.
To go along the 'man made path' will lead to a disaster
But you have called us, each by name, to listen to the Master.
As Jesus needed time alone, to understand the Father's will
So we each need to allocate some time to just 'Be still'.
If we will listen for your voice, if we will give you time to speak,
Then your intent will be fulfilled, through the vision that we seek."

*

BUT WILL WE?

There was a competition in 1995, where we were asked to submit a song for Spring Harvest. This was my effort, with a tune composed by Mrs. Pru Forbes from Bank Street Methodist Church, Ashford.

The song did not win, but the words still hold true.

We will take a stand for Jesus in this world of bitter pain,
Where hurt and fear have crowded in, we'll bring His love again.
And then, when Satan's grip is loosened, Jesus Christ will reign,
For Jesus Christ is Lord.

We will take a stand for Jesus in this world of misery
Where people live with hatred, we will work to set them free.
We'll show that Jesus' love is not reserved for you and me,
For Jesus loves us all.

We will take a stand for Jesus in this world of grim despair,
Where men have failed and doubt prevails, Jesus wants us there.
The world won't care how much we know, until it knows we care
For those who Jesus made.

We will take a stand for Jesus, bringing comfort to the weak;
The hopeless and the helpless are the ones that we must seek.
It's only when we act in love we earn the right to speak
Of Jesus Christ the Lord.

We will take a stand for Jesus wherever He may call,
For Jesus took a stand for us, nailed up outside that wall.
We'll take a stand for Jesus - whatever may befall.
For Jesus Christ is Lord.

*

MAKE A FRIEND

At a Full Gospel Business Men's weekend in 1996, Jim Epley spoke about our calling to witness. He noted that most of us do not have many non-Christian friends. If we are not meeting with non-Christians, how can we lead people to Jesus? His answer was simple:

"Make a friend, be a friend, then lead that friend to Jesus."

In this poem, please feel free to substitute 'her' for 'him' where appropriate.

Make a friend, be a friend, lead that friend to Jesus.
Are Jesu's words still true?
Try asking for a glimpse of Hell
Reserved for those whom we don't tell
That Jesus died for them as well.
Are Jesu's words still true?

Make a friend, be a friend, lead that friend to Jesus.
What is it holds you back?
What comes before His stirring cry
"Go! Tell them why I came to die.
Then watch the demons turn and fly."?
What is it holds you back?

Make a friend, be a friend, lead that friend to Jesus.
How can we not respond?
Condemn them to eternal flames
With countless million other names
Who Heaven loses, Satan claims.
How can we not respond?

Make a friend, be a friend, lead that friend to Jesus.
Just lead him to the cross.
Watch Jesus take away all grief.
Then watch the birth of true belief
As happened to the dying thief
Who hung there on the cross.

Make a friend, be a friend, lead that friend to Jesus.
Then watch the Spirit work:
Convicting him of all his past
Whilst Jesus sets him free at last
From sin and guilt that binds him fast.
Just watch the Spirit work.

Make a friend, be a friend, lead that friend to Jesus.
So why don't we respond?
Are we too happy with our lot?
Complacent now with what we've got?
Ignoring those the Church forgot?
Lord, why don't we respond?

*

TAKING JESUS SERIOUSLY

Jesus tells us to go and spread the Gospel. Are we willing to obey?

We are told to take the gospel to the folk who do not know-
We are not given clear directions but are simply told to go!
For people need to hear the word, so that they can make a choice:
But how can they have that option if the gospel has no voice?

We are told to take the gospel to the folk who do not care -
We must always show compassion, which will earn the right to share.
All people need to hear the word, from the powerful to the weak:
But how can the gospel reach them if we will not go and speak?

We are told to take the gospel to the folk who live in fear-
Afraid of life, afraid of death, and afraid to let God near.
These people need to hear the word, and then choose Heaven or Hell:
But will they know, or will they care, if we won't go and tell?

We are told to take the gospel to the folk whose eyes are blind -
Whose 'intellectual certainties' are a mask they hide behind.
These people need to hear the word, to be confronted with the fact:
But how can these folk be challenged whilst we are so slow to act?

We are told to take the gospel to the folk who have it all -
They're the ones who say "No thank you" when we take the time to call.
To enable them to make a choice these folk need to hear the word:
But how can they opt for Jesus Christ, if they have never heard?

We are told to take the gospel, and to make disciples too -
For teaching and baptising is what Christ tells us to do.
The world outside is waiting for the Church to meet its need:
And if we will go where He directs, with His help we'll succeed.

    October 1998

*

THE FORGOTTEN PEOPLE

Can you imagine what it feels like when your life's disintegrated?
When you're pushed into a corner and ignored?
When your self respect is zero?
When you're no-one's modern hero?
And death is all you seek as life's reward?

Can you feel the pain of failure as your ambitions are frustrated?
And you know that others 'put you out of mind'?
Drift through the days, uncaring
With eyes vacant, simply staring.
Past asking why your life is so unkind.

Imagine you are homeless and your future plans don't count
And you feel your life's a total waste of time.
You are lonely and neglected,
Despised, ignored, rejected.
How easy it would be to turn to crime.

From this position look around you at the folk you've come to know
The hungry, the retarded, the insane,
The lonely and the helpless,
The schizophrenic homeless,
And know you'll join them on the streets again.

So now, from this perspective, look at those who walk away,
Who turn their backs on people in their needs.
And remember our Lord's statement
To His disciples as they listened,
"The world will know 'Believers' by their deeds."

So now when you see the hopeless, all those lonely and defeated
The lives where death will bring a real relief.
Will you walk on by, uncaring?
Eyes averted, simply staring?
Or will your actions mirror your belief?

For just going to the 'God Box', singing hymns and choruses
Will pass a happy hour on Sunday every week.
But will 'cut no ice' with Jesus
Whose teaching and whose order
Was *"Befriend the lonely, and protect the weak".*

*

'WHAT IS OUR RESPONSE?'
OR
'WHY ARE OUR CHURCHES EMPTY?'

This was written one evening in 1993, and used the next morning in church. It was not until afterwards that I realised that the theme for the service, taken from 'Partners in Learning', was titled 'What is our response?'

"There's hurts and pains inside me now that I can hardly bear;
There's hurts and pains inside me now that I can't start to share.
I've inner scars from jibes and taunts, I feel them deep inside
And God alone has kept the score of all the nights I've cried.

As I grew up and faced the world I learnt to hide my pain;
As I grew up and faced the world I nearly went insane.
For when I tried to open up I just got pushed away,
And that feeling of rejection is still here with me today.

There's a hurting person here, who's just desperate to break free;
There's a hurting person here, for Christ's sake, can't you see?
So keep your church, and keep your God, if you are all so blind;
I'll turn to drink, I'll turn to drugs; so I can dull my mind.

My life has lost its purpose, I wish I'd not been born.
My life has lost its purpose, just drink and drugs and porn.
What else is there to fill my days, when no-one gives a toss?
I'm just another reject, just another social loss.

I've lost my job, so I've no cash, so you all turn away.
I've lost my job, so I've no cash, just live from day to day.
If I've no cash I've got no pride, I don't feel life's worth keeping:
Even night is no relief, I'm hurting while I'm sleeping.

I've cried for years but no-one's cared. I've no more tears to shed.
I've cried for years but no-one's cared. You've walked away instead.
If God means what you say He does, you'd stop your inane chatter,
And come and call, and stop and talk, but I don't feel I matter.

Don't talk to me of Jesus' death, of how it came to be.
Don't talk to me of Jesus' death, what it can mean for me.
I really need to know you care, that someone gives a damn,
And wants me not for what I've got, but just for who I am.

I want to be accepted, can't you see it in my face?
I want to be accepted, but you've never seen 'my place'.
"Please come to Church and join us, you'll soon make some friends up there."
There's not a hope in Hell of that, if you don't show you care."

*

REACH UPWARDS

At a Headway Day in early October 1996, Rev. David Barrett spoke about the call of Isaiah from Isaiah Chapter 6. He talked of how Isaiah reached up to God in His awesome majesty, of how he reached inside himself and saw himself for what he was - a forgiven sinner -, and of how Isaiah then reached out to the world in response to God's commands, and in the strength given him by that same God.

It made me think....

Reach upwards, reach inwards, reach outwards!
Draw close and gaze on the Lord.
Then look at yourself, and accept what you see -
Through Jesus the past is restored.

Reach upwards, reach inwards, reach outwards!
Reach others in hurt and in pain;
Those victims whose dreams lie smashed in the dust -
And rebuild those people again.

Reach upwards, reach inwards, reach outwards!
Reach all those people in prayer;
But words alone are never enough -
We have to show them we care.

Reach upwards, reach inwards, reach outwards!
Reach those in deepest despair -
Just waiting to die, all hope having flown.
Sit with them, and listen, and share.

Reach upwards, reach inwards, reach outwards!
Then go where God sends you to.
The world is your mission, you're going for Him
And God's chosen vessel...is you!

*

THE USE OF HANDS

Based upon an illustration used by David Pawson in his 'Kingdom Come' mission to Ashford in 1984, the poem slowly grew, finally taking shape for the Ashford Methodist Circuit Festival in 1993. It really came into its own that year when used in a service to send one of our congregation out as a missionary to Romania.

"Father see these worn out hands, the fingers to the bone,
For I have spent my whole life through, serving you alone.
If you will look you'll see the proof, my hard and calloused hands,
From working for my fellow men, in distant, foreign lands."

*"My child I cannot see those hands you hold before my eyes,
For there's another pair I see, held up in sacrifice.
I cannot take my eyes off them, for the life their owner chose,
For they belong to Jesus Christ, and there are holes in those."*

"Father, please, look at these hands, they show I cared for others,
For they are cut, and rough, and dry, from working for my brothers.
How can you turn your back on me, for doing what you ask?
The Gospel says that doing good is every Christian's task."

"My child, do I hear sinful pride, a sanctimonious tone?
You did that for yourself, I fear, and not for me alone.
I cannot look upon your hands, when Jesus' hands I see
With holes from nails that you put there, that day at Calvary."

"So does that mean that all I've done will now be put aside?
All the days I've worked and slaved, and all those nights I've cried?
The people helped, the lives turned round as I went that extra mile
You now ignore. You now discard. God! Was it all worthwhile?"

"My child, have you not understood what Jesus' hands achieved?
And have you heard the gospel preached, but yet have not believed?
For by His death, with nail-pierced hands, my perfect, sinless Son
Showed I want you for yourself - and not for what you've done.

So come, my child, and enter, you have waited long for this.
It's time for you to meet your Lord - and put your hands in His.
And when you feel those nail-scarred palms, those ragged holes you see
You'll understand why Jesu's hands are very dear to me."

*

DARING TO BE DIFFERENT

This poem was written during a Day of Prayer and Fasting in November 1996; the last verse came during a long period of silence when we were 'listening to God'- something at which I am not very good.

The title and opening line came from a sketch I saw at Spring Harvest many years ago which, I believe, reflects what we should be.

Daring to be different. Daring to take a stand.
Daring to be used by God. Willing to change this land.
Daring to stand up for truth -
That Jesus died for old, for youth;
That lives transformed is God's desire
And in His strength we'll never tire -
Strengthened by the Spirit's fire.
Because we're daring to be different.

Daring to be different. Daring to lay aside
Things that others strive to gain, and laying down our pride.
Daring to proclaim the love
That led you to leave Heaven above
To set men free from chains that bind -
Whole of body, sound of mind.
And Lord, we pray, Satan will find
That we are daring to be different.

Daring to be different. Daring to hear the Lord.
Daring to spend time with Him - eternity secured.
Daring to ask that we would know
What we should do, where we should go.
The people there are God's own field
From whom His love has been concealed
But now - we pray - will be revealed
Because we're daring to be different.

Daring to be different. Daring to sit so still;
Daring to let the Father speak. Daring to seek His will.
Daring to let His Spirit fall
As we respond to Jesu's call.
Then He will set the captives free,
He'll lead lost souls to liberty
Who'll come - and weep - at Calvary
Because we were daring to be different.

*

BE DIFFERENT, BE HOLY

During our time of worship one Sunday in August 1999, Hugh Burnham (the worship leader) challenged us on 'Being Holy', an issue which our Methodist Minister, Jeremy Dare, followed up on a couple of weeks later.

They both made me think.

(To the tune: "Aurelia" - usually associated with the hymn "The Church's one foundation")

"Be different[1], be holy". God's word is ringing clear
To free His whole creation from doubt, and sin, and fear.
The Church was God's invention, (through Christ redeemed from sin)
With Heaven's doors wide open, to lead the lost souls in.

The Lord above is holy, He cannot compromise.
Each sin that we've comitted, He's seen with piercing eyes.
But through the blood of Jesus we can approach His throne
To stand in Jesu's presence, and know as we are known.

"Be sanctified, be holy", by Jesus purified;
Then all our sins and failures to Satan are denied.
We are God's holy people, we are His chosen ones
Once purified by Jesus, known as the Father's sons.

"Be clean, be free, be holy", through Jesu's blood made pure;
Our past is all forgiven, our future is secure.
God's Church can stand together and thwart the devil's plan
By preaching the world's Saviour:- the perfect, sinless man.

Forgiven, clean and holy, and free from all our past;
We have the Spirit's power to serve our God at last.
Our market place is waiting, the lost are our reward,
But will we take the gospel, and help them meet the Lord?

"Be set apart[1], be holy", the Church must hear the call
From God who made the heavens, from Christ who's Lord of all.
The Spirit's always prompting the Church to make a stand.
To fight against injustice. To purify this land.

"Be "Haggios"[1], be holy"! be like the Lord above:-
Move through this world in power, move through this world in love.
The world outside is watching all that we say and do:
But can the world see Jesus revealed in me and you?

*

[1] *"Haggios" is Hebrew for "Different" or "Set Apart", which is what God enjoined the Israelite community to be.*

PUNCHING HOLES

In 1996 Gwen, myself and Hazel, our youngest daughter, went to Spring Harvest. On the first night we heard Steve Chalke talking about a hospital he had visited in Romania, built for 250 but housing 1000, with 4 children lying sideways across each bed: untouched, unloved and unwanted. We were then challenged to be like the Gas Lamplighters of old, who Robert Louis Stevenson referred to as "Punching Holes in the Darkness".

Punching holes in the darkness,
And turning the tide of despair,
Knowing the heart of the Saviour
For others to know that He's there.

Seeing the hope for the future,
Whilst feeling His tears on your face,
Knowing how Jesus is weeping
For others to share in His grace.

Taking His love to the loveless,
Conveying His care to the poor,
Giving them hope for the present,
And a future that can be secure.

So….! Punching those holes in the darkness -
And turning that tide of despair.
Now! Will you join in with His mission?
Or keep sitting - complacently – there?

*

THE CLOCK IS TICKING

The clock is ticking, hours are passing
How much time remains?
People dying, souls tormented
In Hell's awful flames.
While we're silent and not sharing
Jesu's love and grace,
Satan's claiming his percentage
Of the human race.

Jesus said "Go, make disciples
Of men everywhere.
Baptising them as public witness
To the faith you share."
That command to make disciples
Is for us as well.
The Church's mission, and our purpose:
"To bring folk back from Hell."

    May 1998

*

PROBLEMS, PROBLEMS

No matter what the issue, and no matter what the cause
If you cannot cope with what's to be endured,
Just take your cares to Jesus, then leave them at the cross,
For "These are all *My* problems", says the Lord.

If your home is not harmonious, if domestic life is Hell,
And instead of peace there's nothing but discord,
And the actions of your children are making you despair,
Remember "It's *My* problem" says the Lord.

If you feel your life's a failure, if you feel your life's a mess,
If your plans have been destroyed and not matured;
Remember Jesus' promise "I am with you evermore",
And "These are all *My* problems", says the Lord.

If your faith is somewhat lacking, and if God seems far away,
And you doubt your place in heaven is secured.
Don't wallow in self-pity, don't let the Devil win,
Remember "You're *My* problem" says the Lord.

But when your problems are behind you, and you're walking close to God,
When life's to be enjoyed, not just endured,
Don't bask in your own glory, don't boast of what you've done,
For "They were *My* solutions" says the Lord.

*

GOD'S CHILDREN

This was written for use in a school assembly. It never actually got used, but I like it anyway.

When God the Father makes each child
He takes the utmost care.
The shape of nose, the size of feet,
The colour of the hair.
No detail is too difficult
For God in His creation.
Black or white, or boy or girl
God knows each situation.
So don't ignore another child,
Don't walk away, but rather
See that child as he was made
In the image of his Father.

*

BE STILL AND KNOW THAT I AM GOD

Many of us have favourite passages of Scripture. Psalm 46 is one of mine, especially the first part of verse 10. In the different translations I have looked at it is normally translated as "Be still and know that I am God": I have just come across one translation which reads "Let go of your concerns! Then you will know that I am God", which rather appeals to me.

This verse sustained me through many difficult situations, when all I felt like doing was giving up.

It is often easy to tell others, but in hard times the best - and hardest - thing to do is to realise that God has it all in hand.

"Be still and know that I am God", the powerful voice rings out.
"Fall to your knees, and lift your eyes,
Take in the glory of the skies,
And then, in wonder, friend, arise.
Be still and know your God."

"Be *still* and know that I am God", the gentle voice is heard.
"Relax, dear one, rest in my care,
And let me all your sorrows share,
For I, my child, am always there.
Be *still* and know your God."

"Be still and *know* that I am God", the majestic voice rings clear.
"I made this world, and all you see,
I know your past, and what will be
There is nothing you can hide from me!
Be still and *know* your God."

"Be still and know that *I AM* God", the persuasive voice speaks out.
"I AM before the world began
And I made you, mortal man
As part of my eternal plan.
Be still, and know your God."

"Be still and know that I am God!" Have you heard Him speak to you?
Can you step aside from daily strain?
And give Him all your inner pain?
Then let Him build you up again?
And "*Be still and know your God*"?

*

DECISIONS, DECISIONS

I can only speak for myself when I say that what I write, and what I bring when I preach is more for me than for anyone else.

Written in March 1996, if this poem speaks to you, then there are two of us who have been challenged. I pray God gives me the faith to listen to His answers when I ask Him for His opinions.

Does God guide your decisions? Do you turn to Him and ask
"What plans do you have for my life? What's my allotted task?"
And "What gifts have I been given - which I have kept from view
So I can say, "I'm ill-equipped", and hold back from serving you"?

Does God guide your decisions? Do you come to Him and say
"Whatever happens in my life, please lead me through today.
The day ahead's an empty road, and Jesus be my guide.
Then I'll succeed in what I do, for you are by my side."?

Does God guide your decisions when a crisis rears its head?
Do you lean on Him for guidance, or do you turn to drink instead?
Do you know 'God works things out - for those who love the Lord'?
And that His way brings perfect peace? So you can rest assured?

Does God guide your decisions when the offering plate arrives?
Does He control your giving, with its effect on other lives?
Do you ask the question "shall I tithe?", and boldly give in trust?
Or do you feel that 'giving' is a thing best not discussed?

Does God guide your decisions as you reach those with lives destroyed?
The suffering and the homeless, and the long-term unemployed.
And does God guide you as you ask "Lord please give me your vision"?
Or don't you ask? And don't you go? Or does God guide your decision?

Does God guide your decisions? Do you turn to Him in prayer?
Do you ask Him His opinions? Do you know He's always there?
Do you trust that He will answer? Do you know He hears your call?
Does God guide your decisions? Do you trust Him after all?

*

BEREAVEMENT

My parents were very much an 'Army Family', so loyalty and friendship meant a lot to them both. This was written in 1991 after I heard my mother quote her own mother's words "It's like there's no one left to call me by my own name", following the death of yet another 'Old Comrade'.

"It's like there's almost no-one left to call us by our name.
Our generation's passing, things will never be the same.
It seems that - daily - 'friends we know' turn into 'friends we knew'
Once we were part of a great crowd, but now we seem so few."

Looking back across your lives, see how the years have flown,
Your comrades are now passing on, you are feeling so alone.
The pangs, and pains, of parting are now causing you to weep,
But never fear to shed a tear when another falls asleep.

Your childhood links are breaking, of course you feel bereaved,
Don't try to hide your feelings, though, for we are not deceived.
There's nothing we can say, or do, that can stop you feeling
The pain and sadness, but we pray that you will know time's healing.

It may be hard to take this in, whilst feeling such a loss
But it was for them, as well as you, that Christ went to that cross;
And if you and they have trusted Him, and kept His cross in view,
The Bible tells us, in the end, that they will be with you.

God really understands, you know, the pain you're going through,
When Jesus went to Calvary, the Father suffered too.
Whatever you may say to Him, God will never make a fuss,
And when you join your friends in Heaven, please save a place for us!

*

LEST WE FORGET

Despite being from an Army background, and spending my formative years in an Army boarding school, I had never written anything about Remembrance Day until 1999. Although Remembrance Day has been special for as long as I can remember, somehow November 11 seemed more relevant to me that year.

Once a year we honour those who gave their lives in war,
Who fought and died believing in what they were fighting for.
They believed in King and Country, and in the values handed down.
In England's fields and cities, in her countryside and town.

Some enlisted willingly, with their hearts so full of pride;
Though others were compelled to fight, they battled side by side.
They fought for King and Country, and to keep their homeland free.
They fought and died for England. They fought and died for me.

It's not just the old men we recall, who fought along the Somme:-
There have been deaths in Ireland too, from the sniper and the bomb.
In the Falklands and in Bosnia, our forces too have seen
Death whilst serving England as 'The Forces of the Queen'.

Can we also, please, remember all those families now bereft
Where death has taken loved ones, and only memories are left.
The widows coping - only just - on what their country pays
For all those years of loneliness, for all those empty days.

Let us think of those who nurse the shells that once were men
Who went to war with courage, and who were carried home again
With limbs destroyed, with eyes made blind, and minds so full of fear.
Remember war's not glamorous. It cost those people dear.

Remember too the parents who have lost their 'pride and joys'
Who when they first enlisted seemed but little more than boys.
The pain of loss continues still, across the span of years
For although it may diminish, such pain never disappears.

So as we gather round memorials, or simply stop and pause
To think of those who paid the price in just and unjust wars.
Can we think about those living still, as much as those who died -
The orphans and the widows with only memories and pride.

But there is yet a greater soldier, one whose death means life to all,
The One who died in agony, on a cross outside a wall:-
The One who died that we might live, who also died for those we fight.
For it was our common enemy that the Saviour had in sight.

*

FRUSTRATION

I'm stuck in my car on the M25 and the traffic has come to a halt.
I don't know what's caused the hold up I'm in, but I know that it's somebody's fault:-
Some idiot who's run out of petrol, or who's wrapped his car round another.
I'm getting frustrated, and ready to scream, but Jesus says "Pray for your brother".
So I pray for that person through my gritted teeth. That idiot who's messed up my life
For instead of enjoying the M25, I could have been home with my wife.
My dinner's now burned to a cinder, and with worry my wife's going mad.
My children are sobbing their hearts out, wondering what's happened to Dad.
So I hope that the idiot I'm praying for knows the problems he's causing for us:
If he cannot drive, and safely arrive, he'd be better off going by bus!
But then coming from over my shoulder I hear sirens beginning to wail:
My anger's subsiding, my heart starts to thump, my face is now turning pale.
I look in my mirror and I'm sure I can see an ominous blue flashing light -
Father forgive me! And Lord one more thing! Lord please let that man be all right!
Please!!

*

WEATHER FORECASTING

In March 2000 the Methodist Circuit Festival Poetry Competition was based on 'Weather Forecasting'. My mind started to wander to the Bible.

"Father, please Father, can I go out to play, I'm so bored with nothing to do!
It's no fun being cooped up with wildlife galore, it's like living inside of a zoo.
Can I go and play with all of my friends, I'll return when you call me again."
"My child, we've been warned to stay in the ark, for soon it is going to rain
And the waters will cover the earth."

"Father, please Father, can I go out to play, I'm fed up being stuck in one place.
The Nile's been turned red, I've had frogs in my bed, and insects all over my face.
The cows have been ill, in fact all of ours died, then boils all over my skin!"
"My child please beware, my child please take care, the new plague's about to begin
With hail and thunder tonight."

"Father, please Father, can I go out to play, I've been cooped up for hundreds of nights.
I'll be careful to stay in the Israelite camp, not go near to the Midianites.
For seven long years they have ruled over us, so when will God give us peace?"
"My child whilst you play, please check what they say, that Gideon is spreading his fleece -
And the dew will be heavy tonight."

"Father, please Father, can I go to the mount, where Elijah is facing his foes.
The prophets of Baal are ganged up on him - there's over four hundred of those.
I'm told that Elijah will call on our God to show the 'prophets' who's boss."
"My child, if you do - and if rumours are true - those 'prophets' are getting quite cross;
And we'll see lightning like never before."

"Father, please Father can I go to the lake, where Jesus is talking to men.
I missed Him before, can I go to the shore? He may never come back here again.
He's someone I'm desperate to hear and to see - the people will be there in droves."
"My child you may go, and take - for your lunch - two fish and five barley loaves.
And there's a big storm forecast tonight."

"Father, please Father it's Passover soon, when I have to be still and be quiet.
When you were a lad it bored you to tears: Mum's told me so please don't deny it.
Can I play with my friends for just a few hours, the sun is shining so bright":
*"My child stay inside, or better still, hide, for the noon will turn dark as the night,
And then Jesus will die on the cross."*

*

WHAT CAN WE LEARN FROM A DOG?

For several weeks Gwen and I (plus our offspring) had the joy of walking Ben, a very friendly dog whose owners were away on holiday. Ben is very big, very enthusiastic, but very thick. Whatever anyone throws for him he will chase and pick up in his mouth - the bigger the object, the more he likes it. Once he has it (a ball, a stick, a slipper or whatever happens to be the current 'toy'), he shows it off to all and sundry, but keeps a firm hold of it. What makes his day, however, is to collect and carry three or four things at once - he won't put any of them down until the load becomes too big even for *his* mouth, and then he drops the lot, ready for the game to start again.

Are you like Ben? If anything is 'on offer' to be done, do you enthusiastically run after it, and pick it up, keeping it to yourself? If another task comes along, do you take that on board as well, then another... until even *you* can't cope, at which point you unload the whole lot, leaving others to pick up the pieces. After a short while, however, you get back on the treadmill, and start to collect jobs like others collect trophies.

I am reminded of what Mary said to the servants at the wedding in Caana, "*Whatever* He says to you, do it!", and, by implication, "What He doesn't say, don't do", and also of God's voice at the Transfiguration "This is my beloved Son, *Listen* to Him."

God doesn't give us the jobs we are equipped for, but He equips us for the jobs He gives us. If we do only that which He tells us to do, we will succeed, but if we don't listen to God, and obey Him, we will pick up and hold on to jobs which are best left for others. In doing this we will reduce our effectiveness, we will put ourselves and our families under strain, and at the same time reduce the opportunities for others to develop.

Listen, and obey!

*

THE CHRISTIAN FROG

This was the first thing I wrote that found its way into print, whilst I was unemployed way back in 1982. I will always be grateful to those who produced our church magazine in Chippenham.

In the beginning there was a large fish pond, full of frogs' eggs, just drifting around, These eggs were technically alive, in that they had the potential for full life, but did not have life for themselves. Apparently inert, no good to anyone but - equally - no danger either, they just existed, drifting, cocooned from the outside world and the elements by their layer of jelly, which kept their life-potential isolated from the real world around them.

Most, but not all, of these eggs developed into small tadpoles. As tadpoles they had life. They could swim, move, eat and live. Unfortunately this life brought danger, and so a reduction in numbers. The danger came from without (predators found them more appetising now they were alive) and from within (because living creatures can choose what to do and where to go, and some chose the wrong things and places.)

As I said, not all the small tadpoles grew into bigger ones, many fell by the wayside, but those that did found the new life even more exhilarating. Stronger, faster, more alive than before, with more freedom. Sad to relate, not even the promise of further development into fully fledged frogs could prevent a further decline in numbers: many tadpoles could not overcome the temptations, distractions and problems so could not survive to the final metamorphosis.

For those who could take this step, however, life really began in earnest. They were new creations, they were able to move into new areas and places previously undreamed of (can you recall seeing a tadpole hop across a lily-pad?), and they had new powers of breathing fresh air, filling their lungs with oxygen, and revelling in the extra energy it gave them compared with the filtered stuff from their restricted life in the pond. What was really important, however, was that they were the ones from whom the next generation of eggs, tadpoles, and frogs emanated:- it is, after all, only the fully mature that can give life to the next generation. Soon the pond was full of the sound of happy croaking, and, within a few years, it became so full that some happily-croaking frogs had to leave to populate other ponds, previously untenanted, and fill them with happy croaking.

Let us examine ourselves as Christian frogs. Where do we fit in the pond? Our world is full of potential Christians (eggs), with their potential for life in Jesus so often hidden by a jelly-like layer of inertia - <u>our</u> inertia in not sharing the Gospel of Jesus with them. They often do no harm, and so are ignored, their potential kept well protected from bursting forth until the Gospel actually reaches them.

With the news of Jesus, a number will awake to an extent, and, like small tadpoles, experience some life or purpose. It is now that the problems arise: so often the Gospel of Jesus has no grounding in people's lives because the devil sends temptation to distract them from it, and because people, of their own volition, turn from it. If we are faithful, however, we are given life by Jesus as we grow in Him; life forever, and not at the mercy of the world.

Despite this, there is still a fall-off rate among fledgling Christians. Where growth occurs unchecked, however, it is a wonderful experience, preparing us for the final metamorphosis into the finished article, the mature, Spirit filled frog ...sorry, Christian. This is the fully alive, free, living, mature person, filled with the Holy Spirit, and able to do, in His power, things that we previously could not do. These people are those who, by their example, lives, witness, enthusiasm, and sheer joy in Jesus and His promises, are able to bring others to Him, and to nurture those who are seeking Jesus and wishing to grow in Him, enabling His Church to grow.

Where are you? Are you a Christian egg, or a Christian tadpole, or a Christian frog? What do you want to be? To twist a phrase, - "Come on out, the land is lovely". But remember only frogs can go on land: so become a Spirit filled frog - it is what God wants.

*

KEYS FOR CHRISTIAN LIVING

Some time ago I was called upon to give a talk on Housekeeping and Hygiene at work. I used a film "The Key to Cleanliness" to illustrate my points - this film develops the arguments presented as:

K= Keep clean
E = Eyes open
Y= Your responsibility

which puts the emphasis regarding hygiene where it really starts - at each individual person.

If someone was to ask me for "The Key to Christian Living" I think I would have to go along similar lines:

K = Keep praying
E = Ears open for God's reply to you
Y = Your responsibility.

I feel very strongly that prayer is not only our privilege, it is our duty and our responsibility. Jesus never said "if you pray" - instead He said "when you pray". Like so much of His teaching this is not based on "Do it if you feel like it", but on "Do it because it is good for you." Jesus knows that, without prayer, our relationship with God and therefore our ability to live as Christians, will dwindle into non-existence. Satan knows that too.

C.S.Lewis (in The Screwtape Letters) told of the devil asking three of his minions how to stop Christians believing. Having rejected the first two suggestions - telling them that there was no God, and telling them not to pray - (Satan knew that Christians are too intelligent to fall for those lies) he gladly accepted the third one - to tell them that they *must* pray, but not to do so yet.

If we delay or postpone prayer, then we will get out of the habit - and as prayer was a habit for Jesus then it should surely be so for us, which is one reason Jesus insisted that we pray. Satan is expert at wriggling between us and God, making us feel cut off from His love and power. It is our responsibility to ensure that we do not give him the opportunity he seeks. We can do this by praying.

One way of really spiking Satan's guns is to use another Key to Christian Living:-

K= Keep praising.
E = Each prayer is heard in Heaven.
Y= Your prayers will be answered.

When we pray in the will of Jesus, He has promised that He and His Father will answer our prayers - and it is the repeated answers to our prayers that will reinforce our desire to pray. If we get out of the habit of praying, then God cannot answer us, so we lose our desire to pray even more - it is a vicious circle from which we must break out if we are in, and into which we must strive to avoid falling.

One slight word of warning, however, comes with a third Key to Christian Living. When you pray, God will answer, but maybe not answer in the way you want; He may ask you to do something towards the situation. I am often reminded of a quotation repeated to us by an old friend, Andrew Pugh: "I should never pray unless I am prepared to let God use me as the answer." Bearing that in mind:

K= Keep praying
E= Expect answers
Y= You may be that answer.

So there we have it, a small bunch of keys for a Christian to carry around with him, hopefully they may enable you to open a few doors in your life.

*

ENTERING THE CHURCH

This sat on my computer for over a year waiting to be finished. I then read it, and realised I had no more to add - it said all I believe needs to be said.

At a ' valedictory service` in August 1999 for Margaret Adams, who was leaving to go to Ministerial training, the wife of a Minister in Ashford asked for a copy for their church: that confirmed to me that I could put it forward as complete.

When you enter the house of God today,
Please take your seat, and think, and pray.
Pray for the church, for those who lead;
That in God's way they will succeed.
Pray for those in deep despair,
Who no longer have the strength to care.
Pray for yourself, that you will hear
The Father speaking loud and clear.
And when you've heard what He would say,
He'll give you the courage to obey.

*

THE TOOTH, THE WHOLE TOOTH AND NOTHING BUT THE TOOTH

I had to visit the Dentist recently for what I expected was merely to be a check up. Unfortunately it was not so simple, and I heard the dreadful words "Now this won't hurt a bit ..."

As I sat there, mouth slowly numbing with the effect of the anaesthetic, I contemplated my two courses of action:-
        a) Panic.
        b) Don't panic.
And I decided that, on reflection, the latter was a more appropriate course to adopt.

I don't know about you, but I find that with a wide open, numb, mouth, and with a lady approaching, armed (to the teeth?) with an assortment of pliers, mirrors, drills, etc., I find that the best thing to do is to think of other things. I sat and ruminated about the complexity of the human tooth, it seemed a good thing to do at the time! A tooth has several layers, with its own blood and nerve supply, and is held in the gum in a way that allows the tooth to be compressed safely, and still allows good chewing of food. It also occurred to me that there were holes in my gum of exactly the right size for the tooth that was positioned there. Almost as if by design.

My mind wandered a bit further and I dwelt, lovingly, on the ideal arrangement of the teeth of animals. How silly the teeth of a tiger would look in a rabbit (not only the problem of size, although that would be a consideration) and vice versa, each animal's teeth being ideally suited to its dietary choice. Almost as if by design.

I then heard myself talking to an agnostic about God; did He or did He not exist? I heard myself open the conversation;

Me: "You have just had false teeth fitted, I believe."

He: "Yes."

Me: "Tell me about them. Please describe them."

He: "They are white, with pink gums, made of High-tensile plastic - and they fit, after a fashion."

Me: "Did they just appear out of nowhere?"

He: "Of course not, someone had to measure me, design the teeth to fit (almost), mould the teeth from the plastic, and check for faults."

Me: "What about your natural teeth? Could you please describe them, and their history to me."

He: "Ideally positioned, sensitive to pain, they were an indispensable part of my body, growing when I was younger; they fitted better than my false teeth do, as well."

Me: "Did they happen just like that, or were they created?"

He: "Well .... er .... um .... er"

It was then that I noticed that another had been listening to our conversation, it was a white coated apparition, armed (to the teeth?) with an assortment of pliers, mirrors, drills, etc., and she butted in to say "Thank you, you can rinse out now."

So I never did hear the end of that conversation. If anyone did hear it, please let me know as I am intrigued to know if teeth just happened, or if there was a design and a designer.

*

"IT'S STUCK!!"

We were having a new factory built at work, which included the laying of new water pipes. For several days a couple of men worked really hard, digging the trench for the pipe: most obstacles were cleared away but some (such as electricity cables and steam pipes) could not be cleared away, instead they had to be worked around and under with the utmost care.

Soon afterwards another gang arrived to lay the pipe - one of the new, flexible ones without joins, so it had to be laid all in one piece. Things went well for most of the operation until the workmen came to a steam pipe that they had to go under, so the whole pipe had to be pulled along under that obstruction. One man was on the far side, pulling with all his might, the sweat was pouring off him and the veins were standing out on his neck, but the pipe would not budge. One of his so-called colleagues was standing on the other side of the obstacle, hands in pockets, saying very laconically "I think it's stuck."

The Church of God is so often like that scenario: people come in and lay good foundations, removing many obstacles and barriers, whilst working around others that cannot be cleared or moved. After a time, others take over the building of the church, or work alongside the previous folk. All goes well at first, and then a problem occurs. Some will be working hard to get things going again, whilst others will stand there, well back from the scene of the action and say "We're stuck", or - far more likely - "You're stuck."

Whilst not denying that we must speak out if the church is settling into a rut, or if it is going nowhere, I would ask you two questions:-

a) Is your church stuck?

b) Which side of the obstacle are you on? Are you stood back, looking on, hands in pockets, saying "It's stuck", or are you on the other side, busting a gut to get things going again?

*

JESUS' LOVE IS VERY WONDERFUL

There we both were, Gwen and I, sitting in our lounge, feeling a little nippy, and tired. The situation was not helped by the fact that we were both suffering the after effects of colds, with all the shivery symptoms that involves. Suddenly Gwen went over to the gas fire and turned it on. From that small, simple box on the wall came a comforting glow, and an associated warmth which not only made us feel much happier but also gave us a feeling that "all was not wrong with the world", which counteracted the self-pitying feelings we had to begin with.

That glow was remarkably like the effects we, as Christians, should have in the world. Jesus, who was Himself the Light of the World, instructed us to be so also:- "You are like lights for the world" (Matthew 5 v 14) - in other words we, that's you and me, must be so conspicuous in the dull, sad, and miserable world outside that we stand out because of our shining faith, and our brightness should be such as to attract others like moths to a flame. If you then read the second part of the verse I have just quoted you will see that we are called to be conspicuous - "A city built on a hill cannot be hidden", in other words, if our faith is to be more than just an inner feeling, then we have to be prepared to let our light shine and let the world see, and hear, that the Light of the World, Jesus, is still around, and that we are the lesser lights through whom His glory shines.

Asociated with the glow from the gas fire was a gentle warmth, in great contrast to the harsh, cold light given out from a neon lamp. This is what we should be, lights giving out an attractive warmth, which not only makes people happier, but also draws them to us, and thence to a knowledge of Jesus. Jesus, the Bible tells us, was wonderful to know; He was like a magnet to all who came in contact with Him (except those who set their hearts against His call), and this is surely what He is telling us to copy - as far as possible - to create a warmth which reflects His love for us, and for others.

Unlike a gas fire, however, the warmth of the love Jesus has for all does not become unbearable if we get closer to Him, nor does the effect die away when the fire is turned off. In the case of Jesus and His love, the warmth does increase as we get closer to Him, but instead of burning us it merely increases its warming and reviving effect on us. Unlike a gas fire, also, the love of Jesus does not depend on a finite fuel supply, which may run out at some time in the next century. On the contrary, the love of Jesus is inexhaustible; we cannot understand the sheer scale of it. As St. Paul said, "There is nothing in all creation that can separate us from the love of God which is ours through Christ Jesus our Lord." It is this that we have to proclaim to the world by being like lights for the world. We will be best able to do this by letting the love of Jesus shine through our lives, and by living, daily, the faith that we profess to follow, and not merely 'taking it out' on a Sunday.

Can I ask you, if you are not already, to become like a gas fire, a light in a dull world, and a warmth that is comforting: an attractive, gentle and effective piece of God's creation, a cheerful focus for many who look to you for warmth and encouragement in their difficulties and their problems?

*

SILENCE IS GOLDEN

(Please note, this was written when both my parents were alive, this is no longer the case)

Silence is Golden! How often have we heard the phrase, and how often have we said it to our children? What, however, do we use silence for? I was on the phone the other day to a friend, and when I hung up my father asked me if there had been anyone on the other end: I think it was asked because I came off just as the washing up finished, but it set me thinking....

When we talk to others, or to God, that is what we usually do - we talk *to* and not *with*, we do not give the other person (or God) the chance to reply. When we pray it is often we who do the talking, almost without exception. At Church, and at home for those of us who pray at home, we usually follow the well established ACTS ritual:-

Adoration
Confession
Thanksgiving
Supplication

I am not denigrating that (in fact I have preached on it several times), but it has recently struck me that there is no room allowed in that framework for listening to God when He attempts to reply to us.

Prayer, surely, should not be like a telephone conversation

between strangers, or between friends, or even like a face to face conversation between friends. It should be more intimate than that. The happiest married couple I know are my parents, who can sometimes sit contentedly with just each other for company, and not feel the need to say, or do, anything. They do not have to talk. By being silent they are each prepared to let the other talk if he (or she) wants, and if neither feels the need to talk they can just look at each other and their silence *is* golden. They know each other, and love each other so much that the need for continuous chatter has gone. It does not mean, however, that they take each other for granted. Far from it, they still work hard at their marriage (after nearly 39 years) by talking and listening as, and when, they feel the want or the need, and they still enjoy each other's company.

That is what prayer should be like;
i) A level of communicating with God whereby we can talk to Him when we want to or need to, and we know He will listen, and
ii) Our being prepared to listen to God when He wants or needs to speak to us, and
iii) A realisation that just by sitting in His presence and looking on Him, we can grow closer to Him - indeed that is often the best way to do so. As with human love the realisation of divine love does not deepen amid noise and bustle; it develops in quiet times and solitude. Like human love, also, this is a state which develops - one to grow slowly towards - it is not a level we can reach overnight.

In conclusion I wonder if, at prayer time, we should stray

from the Book of Acts (see earlier) to the Book of Psalms. Prayer is, after all, both an Old Testament and a New Testament principle. In this case, however Psalms would be an abbreviation for:-

Praising:
Sincerely apologising:
Asking:
Listening:
Meditating:
Succeeding.

and please note it is all a positive routine, not in any way passive.

Think (sorry, Pray) about it!!

*

GOD SPEAKS - IN THE BATHROOM?

All of us visit our bathroom daily to wash, but how many have ever really studied the contents of that room in any detail? Always a sink, often a bath, sometimes a shower - three utensils all to clean us and restore us, all totally disparate in structure, function and operation.

I would like to take these utensils, one at a time, and hold them up to the light, and examine them - starting with the sink; why use the sink at all, why not just use the bath? Both, after all possess two taps and a plug. The sink, surely, is where we go first thing in the morning when we surface, to clean ourselves preparatory for the day ahead. It is also where we go last thing at night to shed the dirt and grime of the day, to remove the debris accumulated since our morning wash, before we settle for the night. Not only that, it is the place we go in order to clean our teeth (unless we leave them in a jar of Steradent by our bed) - teeth that WE know need to be cleaned although it is currently not evident to others we meet. If, however, we neglect to clean them, then it will become obvious to all, and most unpleasant, affecting others as well as ourselves.

The bath is different - it is more leisurely, taking longer to prepare, and when it is ready we can enjoy it. What is more lovely, and inviting at the end of a tiring day than to relax in a hot Radox bath, prepared just for you? To turn on the taps, see the bath fill with inviting, scented, soapy water, and to know it is just for you to wallow in (unless your children like to hop in and spoil the analogy), is glorious anticipation. This anticipation is realised when you climb in, lie back, and let the water cover you. As each pore in your body opens, the tensions of the day, and all your stresses, just ebb away and eventually you emerge from the bath fully refreshed, relaxed, and restored in all ways, ready to face the world again.

The shower, again, is different. Instead of you going to the water, you stand still and the water comes to you, covering you from top to toe (in the case of our shower it is normally with cold water). This can be very refreshing and stimulating, but it can also be a very rude awakening. To get the full benefit from our shower you have to make a positive effort to stay under the cleansing, invigorating streams of water, when often the body will want to move outside of it to 'more comfortable' areas of the bath, where it feels 'safe', and will occasionally be prepared to dangle an arm or leg into the stream, just to appear willing. A good shower will, however, revitalise us, and prepare us to face the world again, feeling like a new person, ready for action.

Now what, you may be asking, has a bathroom to do with a Christian magazine? I'd like to now apply the same examination to the three parts of the Trinity. Just as we visit the bathroom to clean ourselves superficially, ready to face the world, so it is to the three persons of God that we turn for inner cleansing and renewal. We wash at the sink at the start and end of each day, similarly we can turn to Jesus as we wake (to ask for strength for the day) and at bedtime (to unburden ourselves of our worry and strain, to confess our sins, and to be clean). In fact we can turn to Him at any time, he is always there. In our lives, also, are things that we know are wrong, and need attention, but others cannot see them yet - a situation similar to that with our teeth in that the proof of the situation comes later unless dealt with quickly. It is Jesus who deals with our sins, our failings, our inner dirt, before it all spills over into our lives.

Like a Radox bath, the love of God is continually being prepared for us, ready for us to relax in, to soak out from our minds and our bodies all our stress, our worries, and our fears. The offer of God's love is for all, so go on, accept it if you have not already done so, let it envelop you, relax in His loving strength, and all your tensions, fears, and worries will ebb away, leaving you more ready to face the world, restored in all ways.

That leaves the shower and the Holy Spirit. What part of the Trinity is it that comes when we make a positive effort to receive? What part of the Trinity is it that will wake us from our lethargy, causing us to do things which our bodies - if we were to let them - would shrink away from and take refuge in 'safer waters'? Surely it is the Holy Spirit, a powerful, cleansing, invigorating person, God's spiritual shower.

The other point to be made is that as we visit the bathroom in private, so God visits us in private. Others may be present but God always deals with each of us as individuals, uniquely. If we will only take Him at His word we will be cleansed, restored, ready to face all the dirt and grime that the world can throw at us - and all the problems too. No bathroom I know of can give us THAT guarantee

*

TILE ME!! THE OLD, OLD STORY.

Hello.

Let me introduce myself. I am tile number 25, box 115, pattern style 32A, colour white with brown flowers. Or at least I was until recently - but I'll come to that in a minute. Before I go on, I know what is going through your mind; that tiles can't write, but put beside what's happened to me lately, learning to write is a mere bagatelle.

Anyhow let's go back to the beginning. There we was, me and my mates, sitting in our little box in the DIY shop, in East London, doing no harm to nobody, minding our own business as usual, when in walks this geezer (sorry, Gentleman) and buys us all. Just like that. It seems that he and his Father are doing some work and they needs us to finish it off. Apparently they had spent a long time looking for suitable tiles and patterns, and they had decided that we was just what they wanted.

Anyway, he buys us, and carries us back to his home and leaves us in the bathroom - where the work is to be done. When nobody is about I takes the opportunity for a quick look around, although at that time I has no intention of getting involved - I wanted out! But I couldn't get out! When I looks I sees that one wall is already tiled, But the other three walls is covered with old, tatty, wallpaper. "Not for me," - I thinks, "I ain't going there, I won't fit, I'll fall off," and I gets all depressed just thinking about it.

Anyhow, me and my mates stay in our box in the bathroom, minding our own business, while this geezer (sorry, Gentleman) and his father gets to work on the wall they were doing. They says they was doing one wall first and then moving round to the other walls so that they does each bit properly - and not skimp. First they strips off all the old, dirty, rotten paper and exposes the wall below with all its defects. They then gets to work to repair it. This takes time, care, and rough sandpaper. Watching, still not wanting to get involved, I could see that all the cracks (where the dirt and grime can hide) was being filled in and all the rough bits smoothed off. All the ridges and hollows was filled in and made level. Me and my mates heard them say that this was so that when they puts the right tiles in place we would go into a fully and properly prepared wall, and we wouldn't not just be a surface cover up for a dirty and damaged surface.

We was still not very sure what we going on - But we needn't have worried because these guys (sorry, Gentlemen) now started to tackle the paintwork. I asks you, did they have to be so pernickety. They works at this paintwork, sanding, smoothing, priming and painting, so that all would be ready for us to go into a fully prepared area. So <u>they</u> says.

By now , a few tiles were taking an interest in what was going on - but only a few. Most of us thought that these guys (sorry, Gentlemen) was weirdoes, and ignored them. Boy, was we wrong!

Well, comes the great day they starts putting us in place.

No rushing by these two men - they still goes on being very thorough. First the father gets a spirit level and draws a horizontal line along the wall - so He can judge how straight we are, so <u>He</u> says. His Son then draws a vertical line using a plumb line, so we can be set against it to see how we stands up. There it is on the wall, a cross where these two lines meet, against which we are checked to see if we is right. They can tell if any one of us is not right - what hope has we got? Still, the Son paid for us, so I suppose he has the right to check us, and reject those as don't come up to spec.

They takes us one at a time, starting at the front of the box. Each one of us put <u>exactly</u> into place on the wall, the place where he fits best. And boy - are those two careful in their work, even now. It was amazing, one of my mates fell away, and kept slipping out of position. We naturally expected the father to throw him away in a temper - that is what people does we had been told. But no! He just measures him again, against the cross, and makes a few rubs with sandpaper to smooth down an edge and makes him fit better, then sticks him in place again. It was wonderful to see.

By now the rest of us was getting quite excited - this looked good, we wanted to be part of it. Well, the others was, I was getting worried. All was blending and looking good, but I has a crack in one corner where I was damaged earlier. None of my mates knew this, but I did and I knew THEY knew, so surely they couldn't use me - I were not perfect.

The Son says to his Father "Look", he says, "over by that sink, we need a tile with a bit cut out. Let's use this one (meaning me!) it will be easy to fit it to shape". So they takes me and gently cuts me to shape, trying me against the place they wants me until all the rough edges are smoothed down, and I fits perfectly where they wants me. I fits, perfectly, into that space - a space that only me, damaged and imperfect as I was, could fit. Damaged but now with all the bad bits gone, I has a function, a use, and what is left, after the Son has cut away the damaged, useless bits, is perfect for the Father.

I still has that use. I am here, where I was put, into a space only I could fill - after some cutting to shape. I mixes in with my mates in a planned way, over a prepared wall, and brings beauty and order to a wall what was previously old, dirty and decaying. We is all held in place by something that holds us up, holds us together, and stops the whole lot of us falling apart, as well as keeping the grime and filth out of that area that the Father and Son so lovingly cleared and worked on, What is that holds us in place? I'll tell you that another day.

That's it! Cracked and damaged I was bought by the Son, I was lovingly shaped and I am now perfect for what the Father wants.

That's my story! What's yours?

*

DON'T JUDGE A BOOK BY IT'S COVER

I was asked to write a short piece for a Sunday service in around 1986. This, written with my son Neil (then aged about 9), was the result.

Narrator:-

"A certain young man was doing a sponsored mountain walk between Ashford and the Wye Downs, when he was jumped upon by a couple of muggers who duffed him up, took his wallet with all his credit cards and left him lying in a state of disrepair in a lay-by at the side of the road.

Soon after, a member of an Evangelical Church passed by -literally - and said to himself":-

(Holy music plays in the background):-

"Oh dear! There seems to have been a disturbance, and no doubt this miserable object started it. I shall pray that he comes to a position of repentance, and I shall recommend to the Church Council that we devise some activities to keep thugs like him off the street, making the place safe for good living, respectable people like me."

(Holy music turned off)

Narrator:-
"and he walked on by the lay-by.
Not long after, a social worker chanced upon this young man and said to himself" :-

(Posh voice) "This really is a disgrace. There's too much violence and crime around today. We need more resources to cope with our increased caseload. When I get back to the office I shall write a memo to the head of social services demanding that more money be spent targeting this great social need."

Narrator:-

"and he passed by the lay-by.

(loud rock music, loud voice)

Just then bombing round the corner at breakneck speed on their Harley-Davisons was a hoard of greasy haired, leather-jacketed metal freaks. Screeching to a halt, the ugliest one said":-

(Rough voice)

"This bloke's in a bad way." *(music off)*

Narrator:-

"And he went off to get an ambulance while the others stayed with the victim.

Jesus said:- "Who, then, was this man's neighbour?"
He could also have said:- "Don't judge a book by its cover.""

*

About the Author

"The poet long lay sleeping!

It was not until he was almost into his forties that Stewart French first put poetry to paper. It was during a time of feeling separated from God that he first wrote anything resembling poetry. Since then Stewart has found a real release, and a way of communicating to others that which is real. The poems, and prose, which flowed from his pen have been read in public worship in different continents, they have brought pleasure and challenge to some , have opened doors to spiritual and emotional release for others and - on one occasion - one of the articles contained herein helped overcome reluctance for someone to take the step of faith and be baptised.

Stewart has been married to Gwen for almost forty years, and is a member of a small, but loving, Methodist/URC Fellowship in Ashford, Kent in the UK. He has been involved in the wider Christian Church through the Full Gospel Fellowship (for which he was Chapter President for some 7 years), Churches Together in Ashford (where he served as Chairman) and various other, low profile means.

With Gwen he is a father of three, and grandfather to a growing number of children."